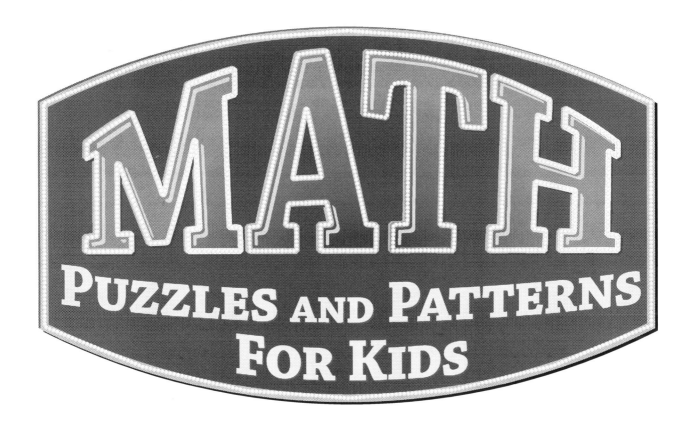

KRISTY FULTON

Routledge
Taylor & Francis Group

NEW YORK AND LONDON

First published in 2007 by Prufrock Press Inc.

Published in 2016 by Routledge
605 Third Avenue, New York, NY 10017
2 Park Square, Milton Park, Abingdon, Oxon OX14 4RN

Routledge is an imprint of the Taylor & Francis Group, an informa business

Copyright © 2007 by Taylor & Francis Group

Notice:
Product or corporate names may be trademarks or registered trademarks, and are used only for identification and explanation without intent to infringe.

ISBN: 9781593632182 (pbk)

DOI: 10.4324/9781003236504

Contents

Teacher's Guide

Are you ready to travel back in time and discover where some of the "big math" concepts came from? The history of math is full of fascinating problems and discoveries. This book will introduce young students to some famous mathematicians and important patterns and problems they studied. The mathematicians in this book were chosen not only because of their importance in mathematical history, but also because they studied problems that could be simplified to a level for elementary students to understand. This book focuses on practicing basic skills within the context of discovering patterns and solving problems.

This book may be used for a group study of math culture and history, or it could be used for independent skills practice to challenge an advanced student. The skills used in this book are based on the National Council of Teachers of Mathematics' *Principles and Standards for School Mathematics*. Students will practice skills from the Number and Operations standard and the Geometry standard, while discovering patterns and relationships in the Algebra standard. The Problem Solving standard will be emphasized throughout the activities. The Number and Operation activities in this book include computational practice in addition, subtraction, multiplication, and division. Younger students who have not been introduced to more advanced computational strategies can still discover patterns and relationships by using a calculator to help solve the problems.

This book is intended for students in grades 2–4, but the activities have also been used with some very advanced math students in first grade. Students may work sequentially through the book, or teachers may select and reproduce certain sections to teach specific mathematical ideas. Students generally will enjoy working these challenging puzzles and may ask for more. Other books related to mathematical puzzles are found in the Resources section at the back of the book. In addition, an Extension Activities section has been included to expand upon the puzzles and concepts in this book. Teachers may also use the answer key located at the end of the book to assess students' understanding of the math concepts.

Great mathematicians looked for patterns and relationships in numbers and in the world around them. They used math to solve real problems. I hope this book will inspire students to look for ways to apply math in the world around them.

Fibonacci Sequence

The Fibonacci sequence is a series of numbers studied by Leonardo Pisano Fibonacci of Italy. The numbers form a pattern. It begins with the number 1 and each number after that is the sum of the two numbers that came before it. This pattern is often found in nature, such as the spirals of seashells, family trees, and the number of petals on a flower. Here's an example of how it works:

$$1 \qquad 1 \qquad 2 \qquad 3 \qquad 5$$
$$1+1=2 \quad 1+2=3 \quad 2+3=5$$

1.) Can you figure out what comes next?

$$1 \quad 1 \quad 2 \quad 3 \quad 5 \quad \underline{\quad} \quad \underline{\quad} \quad \underline{\quad} \quad \underline{\quad}$$

2.) Using the same idea as before, can you figure out what comes next?

$$21 \quad 34 \quad 55 \quad \underline{\quad} \quad \underline{\quad} \quad \underline{\quad} \quad \underline{\quad} \quad \underline{\quad}$$

Other Fibonacci Patterns

Fibonacci's sequence always starts with 1, but what if it started with a different number? Figure out what comes next in each of the problems below. Remember to add the two numbers that come right before each blank. You may use a calculator if needed.

1.) 2   2   4   _____ _____ _____ _____ _____

2.) 3   3   6   _____ _____ _____ _____ _____

3.) 4   4   8   _____ _____ _____ _____ _____

4.) 5   5   10   _____ _____ _____ _____ _____

5.) 6   6   12   _____ _____ _____ _____ _____

6.) 7   7   14   _____ _____ _____ _____ _____

7.) 8   8   16   _____ _____ _____ _____ _____

Try some more Fibonacci-style patterns.

8.)   10   10   20   _____ _____ _____ _____

9.)   15   15   _____ _____ _____ _____ _____

10.) 20   20   _____ _____ _____ _____ _____

11.) 99   99   _____ _____ _____ _____ _____

12.) 41   41   _____ _____ _____ _____ _____

13.) 23   23   _____ _____ _____ _____ _____

14.) 17   17   _____ _____ _____ _____ _____

15.) 150   150   _____ _____ _____ _____ _____

16.) 101   101   _____ _____ _____ _____ _____

17.) 1,000 1,000 _____ _____ _____ _____ _____

Name: _____ Date: _____

Other Fibonacci Patterns, Continued

Solve these Fibonacci-style patterns backward by using subtraction.

1.)   147   91   56   _____   _____   _____   7   7

2.)   105   65   40   _____   _____   _____   _____   _____

3.)   42   26   _____   _____   _____   _____   _____   _____

4.)   210   130   _____   _____   _____   _____   _____   _____

5.)   84   52   _____   _____   _____   _____   _____   _____

6.)   168   104   _____   _____   _____   _____   _____   _____

7.)   252   156   _____   _____   _____   _____   _____   _____

8.)   189   117   _____   _____   _____   _____   _____   _____

9.)   63   39   _____   _____   _____   _____   _____   _____

10.)   21   13   _____   _____   _____   _____   _____   _____

Math Puzzles and Patterns for Kids

Other Fibonacci Patterns, Continued

Now try multiplying numbers to finish the pattern. You may use a calculator, if needed.

1.)   2   2   4 _____   32

2.)   3   3 _____ _____ _____

3.)   4   4 _____ _____ _____

4.)   5   5 _____ _____ _____

5.)   6   6 _____ _____ _____

6.)   7   7 _____ _____ _____

7.)   8   8 _____ _____ _____

8.)   9   9 _____ _____ _____

9.)   10   10 _____ _____ _____

Try dividing the first number by the second number to finish these patterns. You may use a calculator, if needed.

10.)   243   27 _____ _____ _____

11.)   3,125   125 _____ _____ _____

12.)   16,807   343 _____ _____ _____

13.)   1   1 _____ _____ _____

14.)   32   8 _____ _____ _____

15.)   1,024   64 _____ _____ _____

16.)   100,000   1,000 _____ _____ _____

17.)   59,049   729 _____ _____ _____

Pascal's Triangle

Pascal's triangle is a set of numbers made popular by Blaise Pascal of France. The set of numbers is arranged in the shape of a triangle. The triangle is made of a number pattern in which each number is the sum of the two numbers above it. Figure out the numbers on the empty row. Use the hints in the boxes below each empty octagon to help you solve the problem.

1

1   1

1   2   1

1   3   3   1

1   1

1 + 3 =   3 + 3 =   1 + 3 =

Name: _____ Date: _____

Pascal's Triangle, Continued

Fill in the missing numbers on the Pascal's triangle below. Remember to add the two numbers above each blank to find the answer. Notice that the number 1 goes all the way down the side, because it has nothing, or 0, on one side above it. Some of the answers have been filled in already to help you finish the triangle.

Name: _____ Date: _____

Pascal's Triangle, Continued

This triangle starts with a different number than Pascal's. Fill in the missing numbers in this triangle. Remember to add the two numbers above each blank to find the missing numbers.

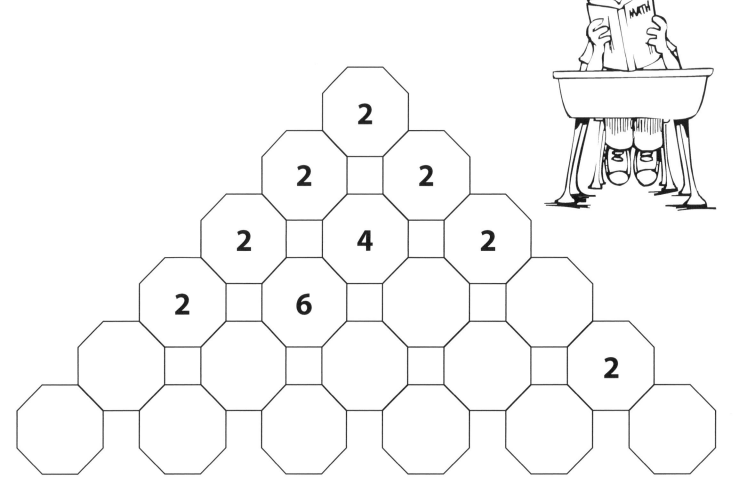

Math Puzzles and Patterns for Kids

Pascal's Triangle, Continued

This triangle also starts with a different number than Pascal's. Fill in the missing numbers in the triangle below. Remember to add the two numbers above each blank to find the missing numbers.

Name: _____ Date: _____

Pascal's Triangle, Continued

Below is Pascal's original triangle, but this one keeps going further than the others we've solved. Fill in the missing numbers in the triangle below. Then, color all of the odd numbers blue and the even numbers yellow. (Odd numbers end with 1, 3, 5, 7 or 9. Even numbers end with 0, 2, 4, 6, or 8.)

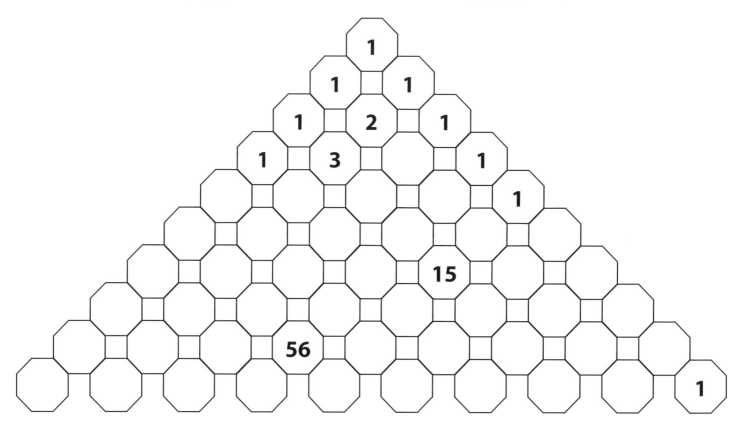

1.) Do you notice any patterns?

2.) What happens when you add two odd numbers together?

3.) What happens when you add two even numbers together?

4.) What happens when you add an odd number to an even number?

MATH PUZZLES AND PATTERNS FOR KIDS

Ramanujan's Combinations

Srinivasa Ramanujan was a mathematician from India. From the time that he was a young boy, he loved working with numbers. He liked to figure out how many different combinations he could use to make a number. For example, the number 4 can be made in several ways:

$0 + 4 = 4$
$1 + 3 = 4$
$2 + 2 = 4$
$1 + 1 + 2 = 4$
$1 + 1 + 1 + 1 = 4$

1.) Show 10 different ways you could make 10:

2.) Show 10 different ways you can make 20:

Ramanujan's Combinations, Continued

Let's try making combinations of money now. For example, you can make 10 cents several different ways:

1 dime = 10 cents
2 nickels = 10 cents
10 pennies = 10 cents
1 nickel and 5 pennies = 10 cents

1.) Show 10 different ways you can make 25 cents:

2.) Show 10 different ways you can make $1:

Magic Squares

Benjamin Franklin was a well-known revolutionary, printer, and inventor from America. He was also very interested in mathematics. He loved to play with magic squares. In a magic square, every row, column, and diagonal adds up to the same number. A row is horizontal; it goes across from left to right. A column is vertical; it goes up and down. The sample below shows a magic square. Can you figure out what each row, column, and diagonal add up to?

8	1	6
3	5	7
4	9	2

1.) Look at the numbers in the rows.

8 + 1 + 6 =   3 + 5 + 7 =   4 + 9 + 2 =

2.) Look at the numbers in the columns.

8 + 3 + 4 =   1 + 5 + 9 =   6 + 7 + 2 =

3.) Look at the numbers in the diagonals.

8 + 5 + 2 =   4 + 5 + 6 =

Magic Squares, Continued

Make your own Magic Squares, using the numbers 1 to 9. Try to make every row and column add up to 15. Can you make the diagonals total 15, also?

MATH PUZZLES AND PATTERNS FOR KIDS

Lo-Shu and the Magic Square

A Chinese legend says that the first magic square appeared on the back of a turtle named Lo-Shu. Lo-Shu came from the Yellow River in China and carried the magic square on his back to Emperor Yu in 2200 B.C. The Emperor took Lo-Shu's square, so Lo-Shu wandered all over the world searching for another magic square.

1.) Do you think this story really happened?

2.) Why or why not?

3.) Draw a picture of what you think Lo-Shu the turtle might have looked like.

Franklin's Magic Squares

This is one of Benjamin Franklin's famous magic squares. It was published in a book in 1767.

52	61	4	13	20	29	36	45
14	3	62	51	46	35	30	19
53	60	5	12	21	28	37	44
11	6	59	54	43	38	27	22
55	58	7	10	23	26	39	42
9	8	57	56	41	40	25	24
50	63	2	15	18	31	34	47
16	1	64	49	48	33	32	17

1.) Use a calculator to add the numbers in some of the rows and columns. Remember, a row is horizontal (it goes across from left to right) and a column is vertical (it goes up and down).

52 + 61 + 4 + 13 + 20 + 29 + 36 + 45 =

14 + 3 + 62 + 51 + 46 + 35 + 30 + 19 =

52 + 14 + 53 + 11 + 55 + 9 + 50 + 16 =

61 + 3 + 60 + 6 + 58 + 8 + 63 + 1 =

2.) Add some of the other rows and columns. What is the sum of every row and column?

Franklin's Magic Squares, Continued

52	61	4	13	20	29	36	45
14	3	62	51	46	35	30	19
53	60	5	12	21	28	37	44
11	6	59	54	43	38	27	22
55	58	7	10	23	26	39	42
9	8	57	56	41	40	25	24
50	63	2	15	18	31	34	47
16	1	64	49	48	33	32	17

1.) The "bent" diagonals in this square also add up to 260. Circle these numbers with a red crayon: 52, 3, 5, 54, 10, 57, 63, and 16. Can you see the bent diagonal? Add these numbers together.

52 + 3 + 5 + 54 + 10 + 57 + 63 + 16 =

2.) Try another bent diagonal:

45 + 30 + 28 + 43 + 23 + 40 + 34 + 17 =

Franklin's Magic Squares, Continued

52	61	4	13	20	29	36	45
14	3	62	51	46	35	30	19
53	60	5	12	21	28	37	44
11	6	59	54	43	38	27	22
55	58	7	10	23	26	39	42
9	8	57	56	41	40	25	24
50	63	2	15	18	31	34	47
16	1	64	49	48	33	32	17

1.) This famous square has another "magical" property. Add the four corner numbers and the four numbers in the middle.

52 + 45 + 16 + 17 **+** 54 + 43 + 10 + 23 =

Math Puzzles and Patterns for Kids

Franklin's Magic Squares, Continued

52	61	4	13
14	3	62	51
53	60	5	12
11	6	59	54

20	29	36	45
46	35	30	19
21	28	37	44
43	38	27	22

55	58	7	10
9	8	57	56
50	63	2	15
16	1	64	49

23	26	39	42
41	40	25	24
18	31	34	47
48	33	32	17

1.) Half of every row and column in Benjamin Franklin's square adds up to the same number, also.

52 + 61 + 4 + 13 =

52 + 14 + 53 + 11 =

2.) What is half of 260?

Franklin's Magic Squares, Continued

52	61	4	13	20	29	36	45
14	3	62	51	46	35	30	19
53	60	5	12	21	28	37	44
11	6	59	54	43	38	27	22
55	58	7	10	23	26	39	42
9	8	57	56	41	40	25	24
50	63	2	15	18	31	34	47
16	1	64	49	48	33	32	17

1.) Circle the smallest number in Benjamin Franklin's magic square. What number is the smallest?

2.) Circle the greatest number. What number is the greatest?

Franklin's Magic Squares, Continued

Figure out what numbers are missing from Franklin's magic square.
Remember that each row and column must add up to 260.

52	61		13	20	29	36	45
14	3	62	51	46		30	19
53	60	5	12		28	37	44
11	6	59	54	43	38	27	
55		7	10	23	26	39	42
9	8	57		41	40	25	24
50	63	2	15	18	31		47
	1	64	49	48	33	32	17

Sudoku

Sudoku is a number placement game that is popular in Japan and America. In Japanese, "su" means *number* and "doku" means *single*. The puzzle originated in Switzerland, but the modern version of the puzzle was created in Indianapolis in 1979. People in Japan started making and solving similar puzzles in 1986. After gaining popularity in Japan, the Sudoku puzzle took off in America in 2005.

The Sudoku puzzle is a type of mathematical problem called a Latin square. Swiss mathematician Leonhard Euler developed Latin squares in 1783. Every row and column of the square must include all of the numbers in the set without repeating.

Let's try an easy version of Sudoku using pictures instead of numbers on a 4 x 4 grid (4 squares across and 4 squares down). Fill in each square so that each row and column contains one of each picture. Each 2 x 2 box must also contain one of each picture. Remember: Rows go from left to right, and columns go up and down.

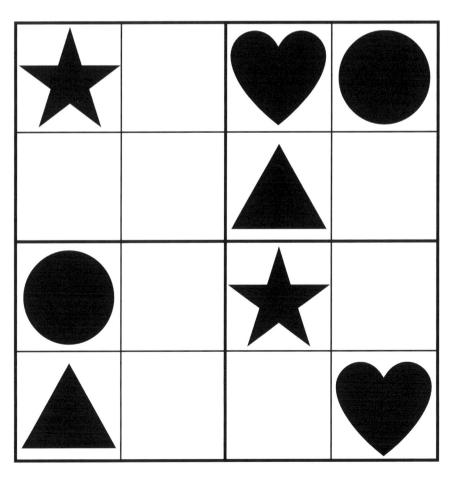

Sudoku, Continued

Let's try a harder one. Fill in each square so that each row and column contains one of each picture. Each 2 x 2 box also must contain one of each picture.

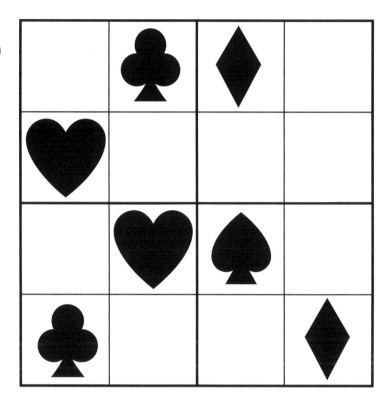

Now, try a Sudoku puzzle with numbers. Each row, column, and 2 x 2 box must contain the digits 1–4.

1	2		4
3	4		1
4	3		2

Sudoku, Continued

This Sudoku puzzle has six squares in each row and column. Each 3 x 3 box must contain the digits 1–9. Each number cannot appear in a row or column more than once.

	5	6	8		7
8		7		1	2
3	1	2	4		
1		3		6	5
9	7	8		3	1
2	6		7		8

1	2	3	7		9	4	5	
4	5	6		2		7	8	9
7	8	9	4		6			3
	1	2		7	8	5		
6	4		3	1		8	9	7
		8	6	4	5	2		1
2		1	5		4		7	8
5	6		8	9	7	3	1	
	9	7		3		6		5

This is the common Sudoku puzzle. It is 9 x 9 because it has nine squares going across and nine squares going down. It also makes nine smaller 3 x 3 boxes.

The object of this puzzle is to write the digits 1–9 in each row, column, and 3 x 3 box.

Sudoku, Continued

Look at the completed Sudoku puzzle below. Try adding some of the rows and columns.

1.) Add the first 3 rows:

$1 + 2 + 3 + 7 + 8 + 9 + 4 + 5 + 6 =$

$4 + 5 + 6 + 1 + 2 + 3 + 7 + 8 + 9 =$

$7 + 8 + 9 + 4 + 5 + 6 + 1 + 2 + 3 =$

2.) Add the first 3 columns:

$1 + 4 + 7 + 3 + 6 + 9 + 2 + 5 + 8 =$

$2 + 5 + 8 + 1 + 4 + 7 + 3 + 6 + 9 =$

$3 + 6 + 9 + 2 + 5 + 8 + 1 + 4 + 7 =$

3.) Add the numbers in the first 3 x 3 box:

$1 + 2 + 3 + 4 + 5 + 6 + 7 + 8 + 9 =$

1	2	3	7	8	9	4	5	6
4	5	6	1	2	3	7	8	9
7	8	9	4	5	6	1	2	3
3	1	2	9	7	8	5	6	4
6	4	5	3	1	2	8	9	7
9	7	8	6	4	5	2	3	1
2	3	1	5	6	4	9	7	8
5	6	4	8	9	7	3	1	2
8	9	7	2	3	1	6	4	5

4.) What did you notice about all of these numbers?

5.) Why do you think this happened?

Name: _____ Date: _____

Rainbow Sudoku 1

Color each square as directed. Figure out what color goes in each blank square.

Pink		Black	Red	Orange	Purple	Blue	Green	Yellow
Red	Orange	Purple	Blue		Yellow	Pink	Brown	Black
Blue	Green	Yellow	Pink	Brown	Black	Red		Purple
Yellow	Red	Orange	Black	Blue	Green		Pink	Brown
Black	Blue	Green	Purple		Brown	Yellow	Red	Orange
Purple	Pink	Brown	Yellow		Orange	Black	Blue	Green
Green	Yellow	Red	Orange	Purple	Pink	Brown	Black	
Brown		Blue	Green	Yellow	Red	Orange	Purple	Pink
Orange	Purple	Pink	Brown	Black	Blue	Green		Red

Math Puzzles and Patterns for Kids

Sudoku, Continued

Look at the completed Sudoku puzzle below. Try adding some of the rows and columns.

1.) Add the first 3 rows:

$1 + 2 + 3 + 7 + 8 + 9 + 4 + 5 + 6 =$

$4 + 5 + 6 + 1 + 2 + 3 + 7 + 8 + 9 =$

$7 + 8 + 9 + 4 + 5 + 6 + 1 + 2 + 3 =$

2.) Add the first 3 columns:

$1 + 4 + 7 + 3 + 6 + 9 + 2 + 5 + 8 =$

$2 + 5 + 8 + 1 + 4 + 7 + 3 + 6 + 9 =$

$3 + 6 + 9 + 2 + 5 + 8 + 1 + 4 + 7 =$

3.) Add the numbers in the first 3 x 3 box:

$1 + 2 + 3 + 4 + 5 + 6 + 7 + 8 + 9 =$

1	2	3	7	8	9	4	5	6
4	5	6	1	2	3	7	8	9
7	8	9	4	5	6	1	2	3
3	1	2	9	7	8	5	6	4
6	4	5	3	1	2	8	9	7
9	7	8	6	4	5	2	3	1
2	3	1	5	6	4	9	7	8
5	6	4	8	9	7	3	1	2
8	9	7	2	3	1	6	4	5

4.) What did you notice about all of these numbers?

5.) Why do you think this happened?

Rainbow Sudoku 1

Color each square as directed. Figure out what color goes in each blank square.

Pink		Black	Red	Orange	Purple	Blue	Green	Yellow
Red	Orange	Purple	Blue		Yellow	Pink	Brown	Black
Blue	Green	Yellow	Pink	Brown	Black	Red		Purple
Yellow	Red	Orange	Black	Blue	Green		Pink	Brown
Black	Blue	Green	Purple		Brown	Yellow	Red	Orange
Purple	Pink	Brown	Yellow		Orange	Black	Blue	Green
Green	Yellow	Red	Orange	Purple	Pink	Brown	Black	
Brown		Blue	Green	Yellow	Red	Orange	Purple	Pink
Orange	Purple	Pink	Brown	Black	Blue	Green		Red

Rainbow Sudoku 2

Color each square as directed. Figure out what color goes in each blank square.

	Green	Yellow	Red		Purple	Pink	Brown	Black
Pink			Blue	Green	Yellow	Red	Orange	Purple
Red	Orange	Purple	Pink	Brown	Black		Green	
	Blue	Green	Yellow	Red	Orange	Purple	Pink	
Purple		Brown	Black	Blue	Green	Yellow	Red	Orange
Yellow		Orange		Pink	Brown	Black	Blue	
Brown		Blue	Green	Yellow	Red	Orange	Purple	
Orange	Purple	Pink	Brown	Black	Blue	Green	Yellow	
Green	Yellow		Orange		Pink	Brown	Black	

Tangrams

Tangrams are ancient puzzles from China. A tangram is a square that is cut into seven pieces. Each piece is called a *tan*, and the tans consist of two small triangles, one medium triangle, two large triangles, a square, and a parallelogram. Tangrams are often used in storytelling. To make a picture, all seven tans must be used and they must all touch, but not overlap.

Look at the shapes in the tangram below.

Color the square yellow, the triangles red, and the parallelogram blue.

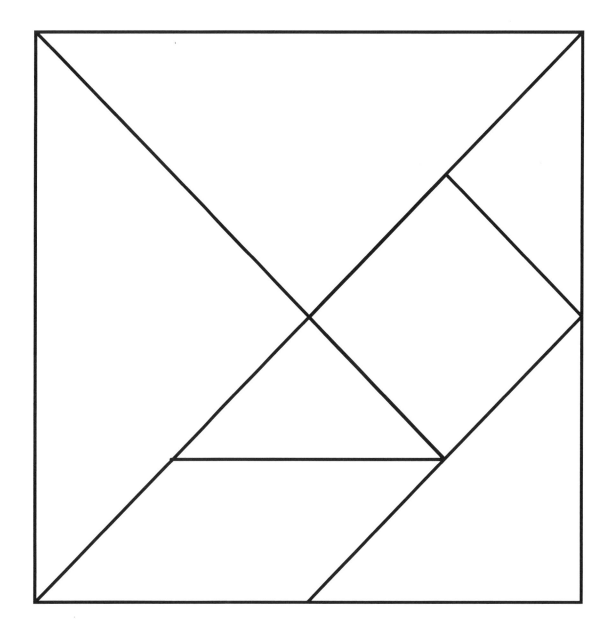

MATH PUZZLES AND PATTERNS FOR KIDS

Tangrams

Cut apart the shapes in this tangram and use them to answer the questions on the next pages.

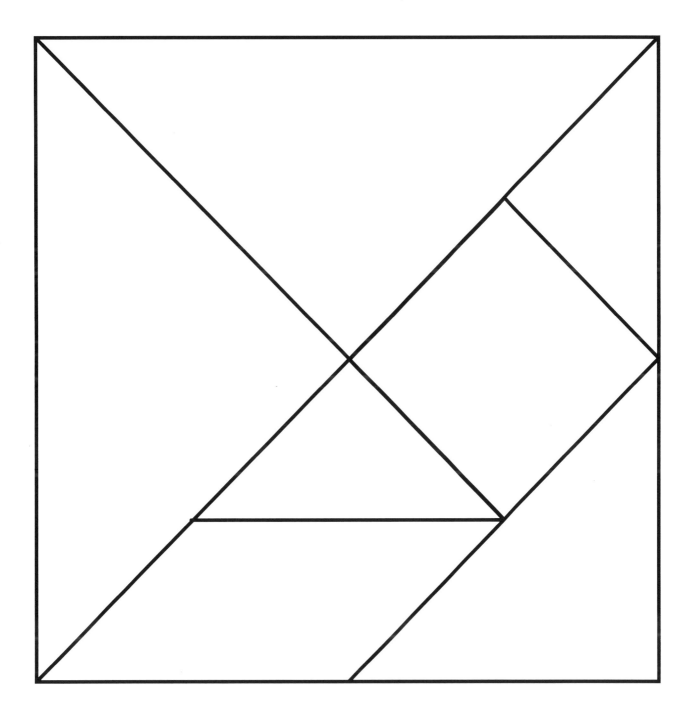

Tangrams, Continued

1.) The two large triangles are congruent. *Congruent* means exactly the same size and shape. Put one of the large triangles on top of the other large triangle to check. Are they exactly the same size and shape?

2.) Are the two small triangles congruent?

3.) Try to make new triangles by putting some or all of the tans together. Draw pictures of the different ways you can make triangles with your pieces in the space below.

Math Puzzles and Patterns for Kids

Name: _____ Date: _____

Name: _____ Date: _____

Tangrams, Continued

Now try using your tans to create rectangular shapes. Draw pictures of the different ways you can make rectangles with your pieces in the space below.

Name: _____ Date: _____

Tangrams, Continued

Can you also use your tans to make squares? Draw pictures to show how you made squares using your tangram pieces in the space below.

MATH PUZZLES AND PATTERNS FOR KIDS

Name: _____ Date: _____

Tangrams, Continued

Can you put all of the pieces of your Tangram back together to form one large square?

Draw a picture of what your square looks like in the space below.

Tangrams, Continued

How many different things can you make using all of your tangram pieces? Use your imagination and have fun. List and draw pictures of the other shapes and objects you can make with your tans in the space below.

The Importance of Being Nothing

The Maya peoples of Mexico and Guatemala were one of the first cultures to discover and use the number and property zero. One of the Mayan symbols for zero was an empty oyster shell. Zero represented nothing and it also represented the place value of a number. Without 0, what would 3–3 equal? Would 10 still be 10 without the 0?

1.) Try some equations using zero:

$$4 + 0 = \qquad\qquad 17 + 0 = \qquad\qquad 58 + 0 =$$

$$679 + 0 = \qquad\qquad 1{,}230 + 0 = \qquad\qquad 24{,}509 + 0 =$$

$$0 + 5 = \qquad\qquad 0 + 13 = \qquad\qquad 0 + 87 =$$

$$0 + 219 = \qquad\qquad 0 + 4{,}065 = \qquad\qquad 0 + 71{,}593 =$$

2.) What always happens when you add with zero?

3.) Subtract with 0:

$$5 - 0 = \qquad\qquad 17 - 0 = \qquad\qquad 83 - 0 =$$

$$957 - 0 = \qquad\qquad 1{,}453 - 0 = \qquad\qquad 7{,}980 - 0 =$$

$$452 - 0 = \qquad\qquad 111 - 0 = \qquad\qquad 1{,}986{,}231 - 0 =$$

$$9{,}700{,}000 - 0 =$$

4.) What always happens when you subtract zero?

The Importance of Being Nothing, Continued

1.) Now try multiplying by zero.

$7 \times 0 =$ $0 \times 9 =$ $18 \times 0 =$

$0 \times 12 =$ $97 \times 0 =$ $0 \times 84 =$

$196 \times 0 =$ $0 \times 521 =$ $3{,}692 \times 0 =$

$0 \times 9{,}541 =$ $48{,}792 \times 0 =$ $0 \times 82{,}309 =$

2.) What always happens when you multiply with zero?

3.) Use your calculator to try dividing with zero. What happens?

4.) Can you divide a set of nothing into different sets? Can you divide a number into no sets?

5.) Here is one more puzzling fact about zero for you to think about. Does zero always mean nothing? For example, if the temperature outside is 0 degrees, does that mean there is no temperature? If a telephone number has a 0 in it, does that mean you don't dial a number? Can you think of other times when zero means more than nothing?

Sacred Numbers

The Sioux Indians of North America believed that four and seven were sacred numbers. They noticed many groups of four in the world around them. They believed the four things above the earth were the sky, sun, moon, and stars. The four parts of everything that grows from the ground were the roots, stem, leaves, and fruit. The four stages of life were infancy, childhood, adulthood, and old age. There were seven divisions of the Sioux Indians, and they celebrated seven sacred rites.

1.) What is 4 x 7?

The answer is 28, thus the number 28 also was special for the Sioux. Their Sun Dance Lodge was built from 28 poles. The cycle of the moon is 28 days, which was the number of days in their months. They also usually used 28 feathers in their war bonnets.

2.) List all of the things you can think of that come in groups of four. (For example, there are four seasons and there are four tires on a car.)

3.) List all of the things you can think of that come in groups of seven. (For example, there are seven days in a week and seven colors in the rainbow.)

Faster Facts

Before the invention of calculators or computers, mathematicians searched for ways to make computations quicker and easier. John Napier, of Scotland, created logarithms to speed up numerical computation processes. We can look for patterns to help us figure out facts faster, too.

Nines

1.) Answer the following equations:

$9 + 0 =$ $9 + 1 =$ $9 + 2 =$

$9 + 3 =$ $9 + 4 =$ $9 + 5 =$

$9 + 6 =$ $9 + 7 =$ $9 + 8 =$

$9 + 9 =$

2.) What pattern do you notice when you add a number to 9?

3.) Try reversing an equation. What's 0 + 9? What's 8 + 9?

4.) Does it matter if 9 is the first or second number you add? Why or why not?

Faster Facts, Continued

1.) Now watch for patterns as you multiply with 9's.

$9 \times 1 =$	$1 \times 9 =$
$9 \times 2 =$	$2 \times 9 =$
$9 \times 3 =$	$3 \times 9 =$
$9 \times 4 =$	$4 \times 9 =$
$9 \times 5 =$	$5 \times 9 =$
$9 \times 6 =$	$6 \times 9 =$
$9 \times 7 =$	$7 \times 9 =$
$9 \times 8 =$	$8 \times 9 =$
$9 \times 9 =$	$9 \times 9 =$
$9 \times 10 =$	$10 \times 9 =$

2.) What patterns do you notice?

3.) Can a pattern help you remember the answers for multiples of 9?

Faster Facts, Continued

Ones

1.) Answer the following equations:

$$1 \times 1=$$

$$11 \times 11=$$

$$111 \times 111=$$

$$1,111 \times 1,111=$$

$$11,111 \times 11,111=$$

$$111,111 \times 111,111=$$

$$1,111,111 \times 1,111,111=$$

$$11,111,111 \times 11,111,111=$$

$$111,111,111 \times 111,111,111=$$

2.) What patterns do you notice about these equations?

Math Puzzles and Patterns for Kids

Faster Facts, Continued

Elevens

1.) Answer the following equations:

$11 \times 11 =$ $11 \times 12 =$

$11 \times 13 =$ $11 \times 14 =$

$11 \times 15 =$ $11 \times 16 =$

$11 \times 17 =$ $11 \times 18 =$

2.) Circle the digit in the ten's place of each answer with a red crayon.
Underline the digits in the one's and hundred's places with a blue crayon.

3.) What do you notice about the digit in the tens place?

What Have You Learned About Math?

Use the words in the box to fill in the blanks.

Fibonacci	Sudoku	Ramanujan	patterns	magic squares
Lo-Shu	Pascal	Maya	tangram	Sioux

1.) _____ is a legendary turtle from China.

2.) Benjamin Franklin liked to create _____.

3.) There are seven pieces in a _____ puzzle.

4.) Four was a special number to the _____.

5.) _____ studied the series of numbers 1, 1, 2, 3, 5, 8, 13.

6.) _____ is a puzzle similar to a magic square.

7.) _____ studied a triangle with special number properties.

8.) The _____ knew that zero was an important number.

9.) _____ studied different combinations of numbers.

10.) _____ appear in many mathematical puzzles.

Resources

Adler, A. (n.d.). *What is a magic square?* Retrieved September 18, 2006, from http://mathforum.org/alejandre/magic.square/adler/adler.whatsquare.html

Alejandre, S. (n.d.). *Ben Franklin classroom activity.* Retrieved September 18, 2006, from http://mathforum.org/alejandre/magic.square/ben1.html

Chevron Corp. (2006). *History of Sudoku.* Retrieved May 31, 2006, from http://sudokudaily.net/history.php

Fitzgerald, T. R. (2006). *Math dictionary for kids.* Waco, TX: Prufrock Press.

Halder, B. (2002). *Sacred shapes, numbers and colours.* Retrieved June 2, 2006, from http//www.lakotaarchives.com/laksymbolpr.html

Hulme, J. N. (2005). *Wild Fibonacci: Nature's secret code revealed.* Berkeley, CA: Tricycle Press.

Knott, R. (2006). *The Fibonacci numbers and golden section.* Retrieved May 15, 2006, from http://www.mcs.surrey.ac.uk/Personal/R.Knott/Fibonacci/fibnat.html

Maccarone, G. (1997). *Three pigs, one wolf, and seven magic squares.* New York: Scholastic.

Malvern, J. (2006). *Can you solve Franklin's puzzle?* Retrieved May 31, 2006, from http://www.timesonline.co.uk/article/0,,2-2149228,00.html

Murphy, F. (2001). *Ben Franklin and the magic squares.* New York: Random House.

Pappas, T. (2005). *The adventures of Penrose: The mathematical cat.* San Carlos, CA: Wide World Publishing/Tetra.

Pascal's triangle. (2006). Retrieved May 15, 2006, from http://mathforum.org/workshops/usi/pascal/elem.color_pascal.html

Pasles, P. C. (n.d.). *Benjamin Franklin.* Retrieved May 31, 2006 from http://www.groups.dcs.st-and.ac.uk/~history/Printonly/Franklin_Benjamin.html

Reimer, L., & Reimer, W. (1990). *Mathematicians are people, too: Stories from the lives of great mathematicians.* Parsippany, NJ: Pearson Education.

Sioux religion. (n.d.). Retrieved June 2, 2006, from http://philtar.ucsm.ac.uk/encyclopedia/nam/sioux.html

Smith, S. (1996). *Agnesi to zeno: Over 100 vignettes from the history of math.* Emeryville, CA: Key Curriculum Press.

Tompert, A. (1990). *Grandfather Tang's story.* New York: Crown Publishers.

Extension Activities

Mathematicians

1. Have students research an important mathematician and present their findings. Some ideas for presentations include: poster, essay, interview, speech, video, computer presentation, or a puppet show. Encourage students to bring the person to life. Students can research the person's important contributions to math, as well as his or her personal life. What was life like in that time? How was the mathematician's life like or unlike the students' today?
2. Have students label and color a world map to show where each mathematician was from. Notice that math happens all over the world. Challenge students to find mathematicians from other countries.

Fibonacci and Pascal

1. Create a Venn diagram to compare the Fibonacci sequence and the Pascal triangle. How are they alike and different?
2. Challenge students to find Fibonacci's sequence in Pascal's triangle. If you add the diagonal rows of the triangle, the sums will be numbers from Fibonacci's sequence.
3. Research more ways that Fibonacci's sequence and Pascal's triangle are used.

Ramanujan's Combinations

1. Use manipulatives to solve the problems. Use cubes, links, counters, dot cards, or playing cards.
2. Use a balance. Put the total amount of counters in one side. Add a few counters at a time to the other side. Record each amount added until both sides balance.
3. Use coin manipulatives to make trades for the money problems.

Magic Squares and Sudoku

1. Use number tiles or number cards and a grid for students to move the numbers around as they try to solve the problems.
2. Make a grid on the floor with tape and give each student a large number card. Students may physically move around and work together to solve the problem.
3. Students may create their own magic square or Sudoku puzzles and trade with classmates to solve each other's puzzle.

Extension Activities, Continued

Tangrams

1. After creating a picture, students may trace around the outside edges to create an outline of their picture. Trade outlines with another student and try to fill the outline to create the same picture.
2. After reading *Grandfather Tang's Story* or *Three Pigs, One Wolf, and Seven Magic Shapes*, have students create a new page for the story. Students may draw and color their tangram picture, and write a paragraph to describe what happens. You can put all of the pages together for a class book.

Special Numbers

1. Research more about the Mayans, the Sioux, or other Native American cultures and how they used numbers.
2. Make a graph of things that come in different sets of numbers. Write each thing that comes in a set on a different index card. Graph all the things that come in sets from 1–10.

Faster Facts

1. Challenge students to look for ways to solve problems in an easier way.
2. Research mathematical inventions that have made our lives easier, such as rulers, calculators, or computers. Students can research the history of the invention and the positive and negative influences it has had on our society.
3. Challenge students to create a new mathematical invention. What types of math problems are difficult for kids today? Come up with creative solutions that could make math easier for us.

Answer Key

Fibonacci Sequence, p. 6
1.) 1, 1, 2, 3, 5, **8**, **13**, **21**, **34**
2.) 21, 34, 55, **89**, **144**, **233**, **377**, **610**

Other Fibonacci Patterns, p. 7
1.) 2, 2, 4, **6**, **10**, **16**, **26**, **42**
2.) 3, 3, 6, **9**, **15**, **24**, **39**, **63**
3.) 4, 4, 8, **12**, **20**, **32**, **52**, **84**
4.) 5, 5, 10, **15**, **25**, **40**, **65**, **105**
5.) 6, 6, 12, **18**, **30**, **48**, **78**, **126**
6.) 7, 7, 14, **21**, **35**, **56**, **91**, **147**
7.) 8, 8, 16, **24**, **40**, **64**, **104**, **168**

8.) 10, 10, 20, **30**, **50**, **80**, **130**
9.) 15, 15, **30**, **45**, **75**, **120**, **195**
10.) 20, 20, **40**, **60**, **100**, **160**, **260**
11.) 99; 99; **198**; **297**; **495**; **792**; **1,287**
12.) 41, 41, **82**, **123**, **205**, **328**, **533**
13.) 23, 23, **46**, **69**, **115**, **184**, **299**
14.) 17, 17, **34**, **51**, **85**, **136**, **221**
15.) 150; 150; **300**; **450**; **750**; **1,200**; **1,950**
16.) 101; 101; **202**; **303**; **505**; **808**; **1,313**
17.) 1,000; 1,000; **2,000**; **3,000**; **5,000**; **8,000**; **13,000**

Other Fibonacci Patterns, Continued, p. 8
1.) 147, 91, 56, **35**, **21**, **14**, 7, 7
2.) 105, 65, 40, **25**, **15**, **10**, **5**, **5**
3.) 42, 26, **16**, **10**, **6**, **4**, **2**, **2**
4.) 210, 130, **80**, **50**, **30**, **20**, **10**, **10**
5.) 84, 52, **32**, **20**, **12**, **8**, **4**, **4**
6.) 168, 104, **64**, **40**, **24**, **16**, **8**, **8**
7.) 252, 156, **96**, **60**, **36**, **24**, **12**, **12**
8.) 189, 117, **72**, **45**, **27**, **18**, **9**, **9**
9.) 63, 39, **24**, **15**, **9**, **6**, **3**, **3**
10.) 21, 13, **8**, **5**, **3**, **2**, **1**, **1**

Other Fibonacci Patterns, Continued, p. 9
1.) 2, 2, 4, **8**, 32
2.) 3, 3, **9**, **27**, **243**
3.) 4; 4; **16**; **64**; **1,024**
4.) 5; 5; **25**; **125**; **3,125**
5.) 6; 6; **36**; **216**; **7,776**
6.) 7; 7; **49**; **343**; **16,807**
7.) 8; 8; **64**; **512**; **32,768**
8.) 9; 9; **81**; **729**; **59,049**
9.) 10; 10; **100**; **1,000**; **100,000**

10.) 243, 27, **9**, **3**, **3**
11.) 3,125; 125; **25**; **5**; **5**
12.) 16,807; 343; **49**; **7**; **7**
13.) 1, 1, **1**, **1**, **1**
14.) 32, 8, **4**, **2**, **2**
15.) 1,024; 64; **16**; **4**; **4**
16.) 100,000; 1,000; **100**; **10**; **10**
17.) 59,049; 729; **81**; **9**; **9**

Pascal's Triangle, p. 10

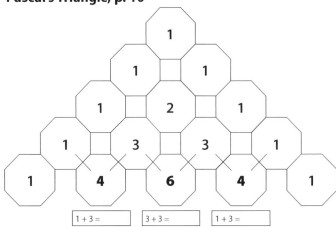

Pascal's Triangle, Continued, p. 11

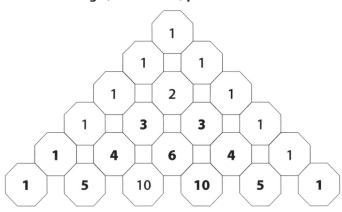

Pascal's Triangle, Continued, p. 12

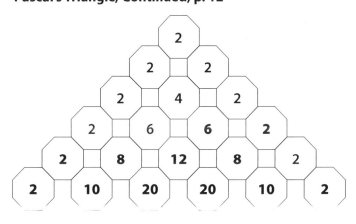

Pascal's Triangle, Continued, p. 13

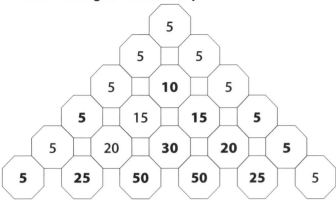

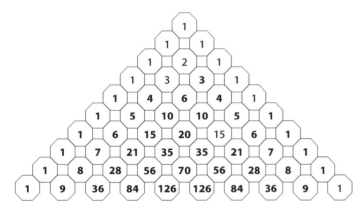

Pascal's Triangle, Continued, p. 14

1.) Pattern answers will vary. Some of the diagonals have ABAB or AABB patterns. Along the outer edges there are no even numbers. The even numbers form a small triangle in the middle.
2.) When you add two odd numbers, the sum is even.
3.) When you add two even numbers, the sum is even.
4.) When you add an odd number to an even number, the sum is odd.

Ramanujan's Combinations, p. 15

1.) Answers may vary. Here are some possible combinations of 10: 0 + 10; 1 + 9; 2 + 8; 3 + 7; 4 + 6; 5 + 5; 1 + 2 + 7; 2 + 2 + 2 + 2 + 2; 6 + 2 + 1 + 1; 3 + 5 + 1 + 1
2.) Answers may vary. Here are some combinations of 20: 0 + 10; 1 + 19; 2 + 18; 3 + 17; 4 + 16; 5 + 15; 6 + 14; 7 + 13; 8 + 12; 9 + 11; 10 + 10; 5 + 5 + 5 + 5; 14 + 2 + 1 + 3; 1 + 4 + 11 + 2 + 2

Ramanujan's Combinations, Continued, p. 16

1.) Answers may vary. Here are some ways to make 25 cents: 1 quarter; 2 dimes and 1 nickel; 25 pennies; 5 nickels; 1 dime, 2 nickels, and 5 pennies

2.) Answers may vary. Here are some ways to make a dollar: 1 dollar; 4 quarters; 10 dimes; 20 nickels; 100 pennies; 2 quarters and 5 dimes; 5 nickels and 3 quarters

Magic Squares, p. 17

1.) 15, 15, 15
2.) 15, 15, 15
3.) 15, 15

Magic Squares, Continued, p. 18

Answers may vary. Here are a few solutions:

2	7	6
9	5	1
4	3	8

8	1	6
3	5	7
4	9	2

2	9	4
7	5	3
6	1	8

6	7	2
1	5	9
8	3	4

Lo-Shu and the Magic Square, p. 19

1.) Answers may vary. Although this story could be based on an event that really happened, it is mostly fantasy.
2.) Answers may vary. A turtle could have a design on its back, but it wouldn't be a magic square. A turtle would not go to see the Emperor. The Emperor could not take the design off of a turtle's back, and a turtle would not search the world looking for a magic square.
3.) Pictures may vary.

Franklin's Magic Squares, p. 20

1.) 260, 260, 260, 260
2.) The sum of every row and column is 260.

Franklin's Magic Squares, Continued, p. 21

1.) 260
2.) 260

Franklin's Magic Squares, Continued, p. 22

1.) 260

Franklin's Magic Squares, Continued, p. 23

1.) 130, 130
2.) Half of 260 is 130.

Franklin's Magic Squares, Continued, p. 24

1.) The smallest number is 1.
2.) The greatest number is 64.

Franklin's Magic Squares, Continued, p. 25

1.) 4, 35, 21, 22, 58, 56, 34, 16

Sudoku, p. 26

Sudoku, Continued, p. 27

1	2	**3**	4
3	4	**2**	1
2	**1**	4	**3**
4	3	**1**	2

Sudoku, Continued, p. 28

4	5	6	8	**9**	7
8	**9**	7	**3**	1	2
3	1	2	4	**5**	**6**
1	**4**	3	**9**	6	5
9	7	8	**2**	3	1
2	6	**5**	7	**4**	8

1	2	3	7	**8**	9	4	5	**6**
4	5	6	**1**	2	**3**	7	8	9
7	8	9	4	**5**	6	**1**	**2**	3
3	1	2	**9**	7	8	5	**6**	**4**
6	4	**5**	3	1	**2**	8	9	7
9	**7**	8	6	4	5	2	**3**	1
2	**3**	1	5	**6**	4	**9**	7	8
5	6	**4**	8	9	7	3	1	**2**
8	9	7	**2**	3	**1**	6	**4**	5

Sudoku, Continued, p. 29

1.) 45, 45, 45
2.) 45, 45, 45
3.) 45
4.) Answers may vary. All of the rows, columns, and boxes add up to 45.
5.) Each row, column, and box contains each of these numbers: 1, 2, 3, 4, 5, 6, 7, 8, and 9.

Rainbow Sudoku 1, p. 30

Pink	**Brown**	Black	Red	Orange	Purple	Blue	Green	Yellow
Red	Orange	Purple	Blue	**Green**	Yellow	Pink	Brown	Black
Blue	Green	Yellow	Pink	Brown	Black	Red	**Orange**	Purple
Yellow	Red	Orange	Black	Blue	Green	**Purple**	Pink	Brown
Black	Blue	Green	Purple	**Pink**	Brown	Yellow	Red	Orange
Purple	Pink	Brown	Yellow	**Red**	Orange	Black	Blue	Green
Green	Yellow	Red	Orange	Purple	Pink	Brown	Black	**Blue**
Brown	**Black**	Blue	Green	Yellow	Red	Orange	Purple	Pink
Orange	Purple	Pink	Brown	Black	Blue	Green	**Yellow**	Red

Rainbow Sudoku 2, p. 31

Blue	Green	Yellow	Red	**Orange**	Purple	Pink	Brown	Black
Pink	**Brown**	**Black**	Blue	Green	Yellow	Red	Orange	Purple
Red	Orange	Purple	Pink	Brown	Black	**Blue**	Green	**Yellow**
Black	Blue	Green	Yellow	Red	Orange	Purple	Pink	**Brown**
Purple	**Pink**	Brown	Black	Blue	Green	Yellow	Red	Orange
Yellow	**Red**	Orange	**Purple**	Pink	Brown	Black	Blue	**Green**
Brown	**Black**	Blue	Green	Yellow	Red	Orange	Purple	**Pink**
Orange	Purple	Pink	Brown	Black	Blue	Green	Yellow	**Red**
Green	Yellow	**Red**	Orange	**Purple**	Pink	Brown	Black	**Blue**

Tangrams, Continued, p. 34

1.) The two large triangles are congruent.
2.) The two small triangles are congruent.
3.) Pictures may vary.

Tangrams, Continued, p. 35–38

Pictures may vary.

The Importance of Being Nothing, p. 39

1.) 4; 17; 58;
679; 1,230; 24,509
5, 13, 87
219; 4,065; 71,593
2.) When you add zero, the answer is always the other number. Zero doesn't change the amount.
3.) 5, 17, 83
957; 1,453; 7,980
452; 111; 1,986,231
9,700,000
4.) When you subtract zero, the answer is always the number you started with. Zero doesn't take anything away.

The Importance of Being Nothing, Continued, p. 40

1.) All equal zero.
2.) When you multiply with zero, the answer is always zero.
3.) When you divide by zero on your calculator, you probably get an error message.
4.) You can't divide a number into zero sets. For example, if you have 10 marbles, you could have 1 set of 10 marbles or 2 sets of 5 marbles, but you can't have 0 sets because the 10 marbles have to be somewhere.
5.) Answers may vary. If the temperature outside is 0 degrees, there is still a temperature. If a phone number has 0 in it, you still dial the 0 on the phone. If a lady wears a size 0 dress, she still has a size.

Sacred Numbers, p. 41

1.) 4 x 7 = 28
2.) Groups of fours include: four-legged animals, four-leaf clover, four directions (north, south, east, west), four quarters in a dollar, quartet, butterfly wings, four corners on a square or rectangle, four suits in a deck of cards (hearts, diamonds, clovers, spades), and four digits in a year
3.) Groups of sevens include: seven wonders of the world, seven seas, seven digits in your local phone number, seven tangram pieces, seven dwarfs with Snow White, seven colors in a rainbow, seven letters in the word *million*, and seven digits in the number 1,000,000

Faster Facts, p. 42

1.) 9, 10, 11, 12, 13, 14, 15, 16, 17, 18

2.) When you add a number to nine, the digit in the ones place of the answer is one less than the number you added to nine. For example, 9 + 5 = 14. Four is one less than five.

3.) 9, 17

4.) No, the answer will always be the same, because you are always adding the same two values together.

Faster Facts, Continued, p. 43

1.) 9, 9
18, 18
27, 27
36, 36
45, 45
54, 54
63, 63
72, 72
81, 81
90, 90

2.) The two digits in the answer add up to nine. For example, 9 x 5 = 45. The 4 and 5 in 45 add to up 9.

3.) When you multiply by nine, you can remember that the digits in the answer must add up to nine.

Faster Facts, Continued, p. 44

1.)
```
                1
              121
            12321
          1234321
        123454321
      12345654321
    1234567654321
  123456787654321
12345678987654321
```

2.) The answer counts up to the number of ones that were in the number you multiplied and then back down again. For example, in 1,111 x 1,111, there are four ones in 1,111, so the answer counts up to 4 and then back down again.

Faster Facts, Continued, p. 45

1.) 121, 132
143, 154
165, 176
187, 198

2.) The digit in the tens place is the sum of the digit in the one's and hundred's places.

What Have You Learned About Math?, p. 47

1.) Lo-Shu
2.) magic squares
3.) tangram
4.) Sioux
5.) Fibonacci
6.) Sudoku
7.) Pascal
8.) Maya
9.) Ramanujan
10.) Patterns

About the Author

Kristy Fulton earned her teaching certification and bachelor's degree in English from the University of Texas of the Permian Basin in Odessa, TX. She has been teaching first grade for 13 years. Her last 8 years have been spent at Whitney Elementary School in Whitney, TX. Kristy recently won a Classroom Innovation Grant from First Choice Power. Her first-grade class also became a Model Classroom for the Reading Renaissance Accelerated Reader Program. Kristy lives near beautiful Lake Whitney, TX, with her husband and son.

Common Core State Standards Alignment

Grade	Common Core State Standards in Math
Grade 1	1.OA.A Represent and solve problems involving addition and subtraction.
	1.OA.C Add and subtract within 20.
	1.OA.D Work with addition and subtraction equations.
	1.NBT.B Understand place value.
	1.NBT.C Use place value understanding and properties of operations to add and subtract.
Grade 2	2.OA.A Represent and solve problems involving addition and subtraction.
	2.OA.B Add and subtract within 20.
	2.NBT.A Understand place value.
	2.NBT.B Use place value understanding and properties of operations to add and subtract.
	2.MD.C Work with time and money.
Grade 3	3.OA.A Represent and solve problems involving multiplication and division.
	3.OA.B Understand properties of multiplication and the relationship between multiplication and division.
	3.OA.C Multiply and divide within 100.
	3.OA.D Solve problems involving the four operations, and identify and explain patterns in arithmetic.
	3.NBT.A Use place value understanding and properties of operations to perform multi-digit arithmetic.
Grade 4	4.OA.A Use the four operations with whole numbers to solve problems.
	4.OA.C Generate and analyze patterns.
	4.NBT.A Generalize place value understanding for multi-digit whole numbers.
	4.NBT.B Use place value understanding and properties of operations to perform multi-digit arithmetic.
Key - Mathematics	OA = Operations and Algebraic Thinking; NBT = Numbers & Operations in Base Ten; MD = Measurement & Data

Printed in the United States
by Baker & Taylor Publisher Services